YoYo Allergies

Elizabeth Beulla

Archway Publishing books may be ordered through booksellers or by contacting:

Archway Publishing
1663 Liberty Drive
Bloomington, IN 47403
www.archwaypublishing.com
844-669-3957

ISBN: 978-1-6657-1902-5 (sc)
ISBN: 978-1-6657-1904-9 (hc)
ISBN: 978-1-6657-1903-2 (e)

Print information available on the last page.

Archway Publishing rev. date: 03/08/2022

YoYo
Allergies

Allergies

It's Nothing to Sneeze About...

Day by day Izzie does everything to help with her mom who is sick. Each day seems to be the same routine, house bound by choice. Izzie's mom is getting older but the one thing that is slowing her down is being stuck in a state of loneliness.

Sure she has Izzie who talks non-stop and begs to get ice-cream on a hot day. After the loss of her mother, daughter, and best friend, it's no wonder, Izzie's mother, Anna, dreads the dog days of summer. One day while Izzie was swinging on her swing in the backyard, an idea snapped after seeing a dog and its owner pass by. "Mom needs a dog!", said Izzie.

In the same week, Izzie went to the doctor for allergy testing. They put all these needles on her back. Surprisingly, it didn't hurt, but there were areas that became extremely itchy. Izzie wanted to have her back scratched so bad she could barely stand it. The itching indicated an allergy of some kind. As the doctor noticed Izzie's legs kicking, he knew Izzie was losing her patience. "Almost done, Izzie", the doctor stated.

Once the testing was over, the doctor carefully removed the wiring and tape off her back, then walked out of the room to gather the results. Within several minutes, Izzie's doctor gave the most shocking news. The itchiness was in fact an allergy of...Cats and dogs. "What?!", Izzie shouted. All at once Izzie's mind was scrambled like a game of scrabble itself. She was trying to piece together what all this meant.

On a scale of one to five, Izzie scored, one, which meant only slightly allergic. This was a relief since she wanted to find a dog for her mom. Once home, Izzie called her brother who worked full-time to share her idea. Not saying a word about the results from the allergy test, Billy liked the idea of their mother having a pet to keep her company and perhaps give her exercise by walking it.

Billy had been concerned about his mother's health and lack of motivation quite some time, but he hadn't known what to do about it. A dog sounded like a great idea, and thought, well, what can it hurt? Then, picked up Izzie. Minutes later, they spotted an adoption sign for puppies.

Billy immediately put his turning signal on and found a parking spot. Nervous with each step, he was greeted by a gentleman who was selling beagle puppies. When asked, Can I help you?, Billy explained how he was thinking about a dog for his mother who was lonely. The man glanced up and smiled. "You've come to the right place."

Billy was overwhelmed by the puppies who all seemed to want his attention. By the roll of the dice, sort of speak, Billy picked out of the litter of assorted puppies.

Once he pointed to the particular puppy of choice, Billy face melted in shock at the price. Then, said to himself, "Well, if a puppy will help my mom, then it's worth the cost." When leaving the parking lot, he debated if he should call his mother and sister, or to surprise them by showing up at their house.

Billy had two options, in which weren't easy ones. He thought if he'd called his mom, she may reject the idea. Or, if he were to surprise her, she may be upset that he didn't ask permission to get a dog. It was a choice Billy had to make. After thinking it over, he chose to do a surprise visit.

Minutes later, Billy pulled into our driveway and carried the dog to the door. After Anna heard a car door slam, she opened the front door and couldn't believe her eyes. It was a black and brown colored puppy. Izzie was standing next to Billy, and shouted, "Hey Mom. We have a puppy!"

As she put her hand out to pet it, she instantly sneezed. Ahh. Choo. Izzie's mom nervously laughed..."a puppy for us? They make me sneeze!" Billy explained how a dog could give her a reason to get out and enjoy some sunshine.

11

As Izzie heard this, she shouted, "Yeah, Mom. Needing to walk is nothing to sneeze about!" Anna chuckled at the sarcasm. Then, Izzie and her sneezed at the same time. "Guess the allergy testing was accurate after all", Izzie stated.

YOYO ALLERGIES!

Yoyo allergies just leave me alone.
I don't like your nasal tone.
Yoyo allergies you stuff up my brain.
You're so annoying, and drive me insane
Yoyo allergies who thinks you're cool,
Whoever you are must be a fool.
Yoyo allergies you take away my fun.
You make me miserable, in rain and sun.
Yoyo allergies, please go away,
So I can have a better day.

allergies

Dogs are special four-legged creatures who know how to be a friend. They, like humans, make messes, get a temper when angry, and show signs of sadness when something is going wrong. Jazzy is a picky eater, yet likes strange human food, too, such as crackers and chips. Jazzy has always shown signs of affection to those come in and out of their home, and is especially loving when not feeling well. It wasn't until change occurred in Izzie's home when discovering how much Jazzy cares for her family, as the family does her.

The winter had come and gone. Not a trace of sickness insight. Until all of a sudden a terrifying virus hit the US months ago, and it traveled into Izzie's home. All at once, Izzie's mom, brother and herself all came down with coronavirus. Izzie had thought before hand, her family done everything to avoid the virus by wearing masks, washing our hands, and keeping at a distance from others. Needless to say, they all still got it. While her brother and she got the typical symptoms including loss of taste, fatigue, chills, and slight fever, their mom's condition was much worse. It is said the coronavirus affects the lungs, and unfortunately, that is how it affected Izzie's mom, strongly.

For those who don't have a dog, it is said they have a great sense of smell, along with being intuitive. This means dogs often notice when something is wrong. Izzie's dog, Jazzy, began going around Anna a little more than usual. When sitting at the kitchen table, Jazzy was right under the table lying under her feet. After Anna's conditioned worsened, a neighbor friend came by and took her to the hospital where she received the care she needed to get well. The first night at the house without Anna was not only extremely difficult for Izzie but Jazzy, too.

15

Dogs experience sadness just as humans do. Jazzy all of a sudden stopped running around the yard as puppies do. She began to leave food in her bowl instead of begging for more. Jazzy also started sleeping more, and lastly, continue to lay under the kitchen table in front of the chair Anna always sat. Jazzy missed Anna terribly.

Hours of staying in the same spot, peering at the front door, there were moments as it seemed tears dripped from her eyes. Jazzy was about a month away from turning a year old. From the lack of motivation, it appeared as Jazzy aged about ten years. Izzie's mom was still allergic to dogs, but had fallen in love with sweet Jazzy, and vise versa.

Jazzy perked up when hearing Nana's voice on the phone. However, after hanging up, Jazzy continued to put her head down between her paws. No one knew when Anna was coming home, so days continued to drag on.

After four weeks, Nana was finally released from the hospital. As the front door opened Jazzy ran towards Izzie's mom, wagging her tail as if she shouted, "Nana is home!"

Anna took allergy medicine everyday but she still sneezed around dogs. Izzie's family believed Jazzy was a God's sent because for some reason, Anna, all of a sudden, quit sneezing so much. While Jazzy enjoyed being under her Nana's feet at the table, she began being around Anna even more often once home from the hospital.

Some may call it luck, others could call it a blessing. Jazzy and Nana sat side by side on a sofa at night and watched TV. Sometimes, Jazzy chosed to lay on Anna's over-sized foot stool, against her legs and feet.

When nature called, Jazzy often followed her Nana into the restroom, wagging her tail, prancing along. Everywhere Nana went, her puppy followed. Above all, Jazzy's favorite place to go was Nana's bed! While the bed was tall, Jazzy figured out a way to snuggle with Nana by jumping onto an empty popcorn tin located between the window and bed. As Izzie peeked her head around the corner, she spotted Jazzy laying in bed with Nana. AHH CHOO! Okay. Maybe once in awhile, Nana still sneezed around her Jazzy girl.

Printed in the United States
by Baker & Taylor Publisher Services